TAVIS SMILEY Presents

America I AM: *The African American Imprint*

Before the Pilgrims landed we were here . . .

We brought—

A gift of story and song—soft, stirring melody in an
ill-harmonized and unmelodious land . . . (Cultural)

The gift of sweat and brawn to beat back the wilderness, conquer the soil,
and lay the foundation of this vast economic empire . . . (Economic)

A gift of the Spirit . . . fire and blood, prayer and sacrifice,
offered before the altar of the God of Right.
Nor has our gift of the Spirit been merely passive . . . (Spiritual)

One cannot think of democracy in America or in the modern world
without reference to the American Negro. (Socio-political)

Are these gifts worth the giving? Is not this work
and striving worth the effort?

Would America have been America without her Negro people?

America I AM
JOURNAL

Other America I AM publications

America I AM *Black Facts:*
The Timelines of African American History, 1601–2008
by Quintard Taylor

America I AM *Legends:*
Rare Moments and Inspiring Words
Edited by SmileyBooks

America I AM

JOURNAL

THE AFRICAN AMERICAN IMPRINT

Edited by Clarence Reynolds
and SmileyBooks

SMILEYBOOKS

Distributed by Hay House, Inc.

Carlsbad, California • New York City
London • Sydney • Johannesburg
Vancouver • Hong Kong • New Delhi

ISBN: 978-1-4019-2407-2

13 12 11 10 4 3 2 1
1st edition, May 2010

Printed in the United States of America

CONTENTS

America I AM
W.E.B. DU BOIS

Would America have been America without her Negro people?

W. E. B. Du Bois—civil rights activist, author, and editor—was one of America's most gifted and eloquent intellectuals, and the leading voice in the 20th-century fight for equal rights in U.S. society.

The question posed by Du Bois serves as the underlying theme for the America I AM: *The African American Imprint* exhibit. It spurs us to consider how the original gifts of African culture were uniquely manifested in America, and helped to lay the foundation for the creation of this country. If we wrestle with this question, we will begin to see just how central black people have been in creating, sustaining, and contributing to America, both past and present. Such contemplation allows us to finally recognize African Americans' indisputable economic, socio-political, spiritual, and cultural imprint.

I believe IN THE NEGRO RACE

"Especially do I believe in the Negro Race: in the beauty of its genius,
the sweetness of its soul, and its strength in that meekness
which shall yet inherit this turbulent earth."

— W. E. B. Du Bois

> "Through history, the powers of single black men flash here and there like *falling stars*, and die sometimes before the world has rightly gauged their brightness."
>
> — W. E. B. Du Bois

Falling STARS

"For this is a beautiful world; this is a wonderful America, which the founding fathers dreamed until their sons drowned it in the blood of slavery and devoured it in greed. Our children must rebuild it . . ."

— W. E. B. Du Bois

OUR children must rebuild it

POWER of the BALLOT

"The power of the ballot we need in sheer defense,
else what shall save us from a second slavery?"

— W. E. B. Du Bois

TWO SOULS, two thoughts

"It is a peculiar sensation, this double-consciousness,
this sense of always looking at one's self through the eyes of others . . .
One ever feels his twoness,—an American, a Negro; two souls, two thoughts,
two unreconciled strivings; two warring ideals in one dark body,
whose dogged strength alone keeps it from being torn asunder."

— W. E. B. Du Bois

> "Freedom is a state of mind:
> a spiritual unchoking of the wells of human power and superhuman love."
>
> — W. E. B. Du Bois

Freedom is
A STATE OF MIND

"Men must not only know, they must act."

— W. E. B. Du Bois

MEN must act

WE will never CEASE

"We claim for ourselves every single right that belongs to a freeborn American, political, civil and social; and until we get these rights we will never cease to protest and assail the ears of America!"

— W. E. B. Du Bois

LIFE has its pain

"Life has its pain and evil—its bitter disappointments; but I like a good novel and in healthful length of days, there is infinite joy in seeing the World, the most interesting of continued stories unfold, even though one misses THE END."

— W. E. B. Du Bois

"I am especially glad of the divine gift of laughter; it has made the world human and lovable, despite all its pain and wrong."

— W. E. B. Du Bois

DIVINE GIFT of laughter

HONESTY,
KNOWLEDGE, and EFFICIENCY

It must TEACH LIFE

"Education must not simply teach work—it must teach life."
— W. E. B. Du Bois

PEACE is not an end

"Peace is not an end. It is the gateway to real civilization. With peace all things may be added. With war, we destroy even that which the toil and sacrifice of ages have builded."

— W. E. B. Du Bois

> "The cost of liberty is less than the price of repression."
> — W. E. B. Du Bois

The cost of LIBERTY

America I AM
ROOTED IN AFRICA

Enslaved Africans were stolen not from a dark world of "savages" but from societies where Europeans traded with diverse West African cultures for goods like Benin bronze and Ashanti gold, ivory, timber, and crops. Living in complex civilizations that included empires, city-states, and villages, African society was rich and varied. Its inhabitants ranged from royalty to merchants, artisans, and farmers.

When Columbus "discovered" North America in 1492, enslaved Africans became the preferred commodity for free labor to build and expand the New World. But in the process, captive Africans brought African culture with them to America, which helped to define this country and profoundly affected who we are as a people.

"Africa is not only our mother, but in the light of the most recent science is beginning to appear as the mother of civilization."

— ALAIN LOCKE

MOTHER of civilization

"... black people marched in the front ranks of the emerging human procession. They founded empires and states. They extended the boundaries of the possible. They made some of the critical discoveries and contributions that led to the modern world."

— LERONE BENNETT, JR.

More than
A GLAMOROUS FACT

"For Africa is more than a glamorous fact. It is historical truth.
No man can know where he is going unless he knows exactly where
he has been and exactly how he arrived at his present place."

— MAYA ANGELOU

"Three things Africa has given the world,
and they form the essence of African culture:
beginnings, the village unit, and art in sculpture and music."

— W. E. B. Du Bois

Essence of AFRICAN CULTURE

"You are the ancient builders of civilization. Before there was civilization, you were there, and when civilization was built, your fathers built it."

— MINISTER LOUIS FARRAKHAN

ANCIENT BUILDERS
of civilization

America is AFRICAN

"The African slave who sailed to the New World did not sail alone.
People brought their culture no matter how adverse the circumstances.
And therefore part of America is African."

— HENRY LOUIS GATES, JR.

THEIR enemy

SLAVES PACKED BELOW AND ON DECK.

"We saw the Moors with their women and children coming out of their huts
as fast as they could, when they caught sight of their enemy.
Our men . . . fell upon them killing and taking all they could."

— THE CHRONICLES OF GUINEA BY AZURARA

"What heart . . . would not be moved by the sentiment of pity on seeing such a flock; for some held their heads bowed down, and their faces were bathed with tears; others were groaning grievously, lifting their eyes to heaven . . ."

— THE CHRONICLES OF GUINEA BY AZURARA

Their eyes to HEAVEN

— PETER WILLIAMS, JR.

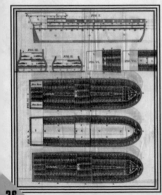

OH Africa, Africa!

Saying GOODBYE

"Imagine saying goodbye to all that you have known—
your family, your children. The screams were said to be
so loud they drowned the noise of many drums."

— FELIX NGUAH

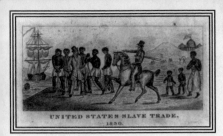

UNITED STATES SLAVE TRADE.
1830.

Not one
LASTING BENEFIT

"It may be safely affirmed that from our first settlement
on the coast until the abolition of the slave trade in 1807,
we did not confer one lasting benefit upon the people."

— A BRITISH OFFICIAL WRITING IN 1853

"They will remember that we were sold but they won't remember that we were strong. They will remember that we were bought, but not that we were brave."

— WILLIAM PRESCOTT

Remember we were STRONG

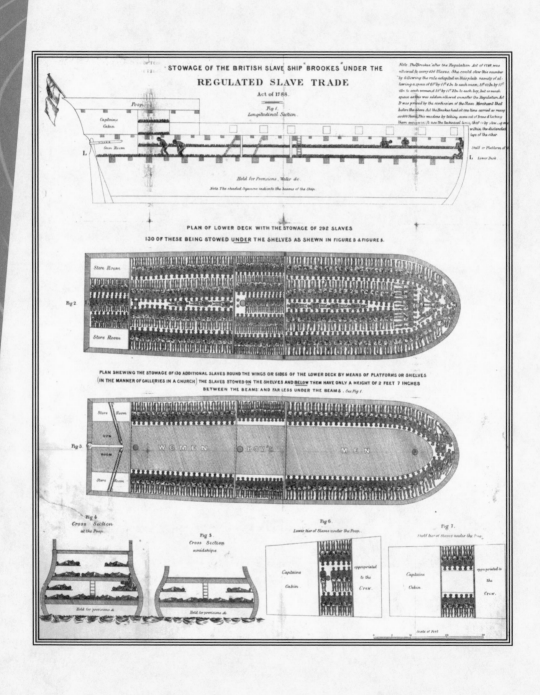

America I AM
OUR FOUNDATION

The socio-political imprint of slavery's inhumanity is known, but enslaved Africans' "loss" of their status as human beings became America's "gain." Enslaved free labor increased American wealth on a personal, national, and global level. America's wealth generated by slavery in present day value has been estimated to be as much as $24 trillion.

Enslaved Africans did the backbreaking work to build houses and forts, clear land, and plant and harvest crops. They had to learn new languages as they worked in surroundings that must have seemed strange and frightening. When the colonies became the United States, slavery was still growing in both the North and South. Slave labor made plantation owners, merchants, and other business people rich.

Institutionalized slavery alone generated enormous economic wealth, not only through Africans' free labor, but also through their knowledge, such as growing rice, which would become the South's major cash crop until the cotton industry emerged in the 19th century.

"When I looked around the ship too and saw . . . a multitude of black people of every description chained together, every one of their countenances expressing dejection and sorrow, I no longer doubted of my fate; and quite overpowered with horror and anguish, I fell motionless on the deck and fainted."

— OLAUDAH EQUIANO

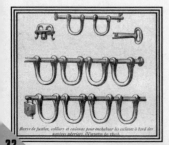

Barre de justice, colliers et caisnas pour enchaîner les esclaves à bord des navires nêgriers. (Vignette de 1825).

I NO LONGER DOUBTED of my fate

THEY CAME with broken HEARTS

"They came not with glad spirits to select their homes
in the New World. They came not with their own consent,
to find unmolested enjoyment of the blessings of this fruitful soil . . .
They came with broken hearts, from their beloved native land,
and were doomed to unrequited toil and deep degradation."

— HENRY HIGHLAND GARNET

CRUELTIES OF SLAVERY.

lak mah BACK SHOLY BREAK

"Wok in de field, chop wood, hoe cawn, till sometime
I feels lak mah back sholy break."

— SARAH CUDGER

"I have heard their groans and sighs, and seen their tears, and I would give every drop of blood in my veins to free them."

— HARRIET TUBMAN

Every drop of BLOOD

"I didn't know I was a slave
until I found out I couldn't do the things I wanted."

— FREDERICK DOUGLASS

I DIDN'T KNOW
I was a slave

Root and branch DESTROYED

"I come from another field—the country of the slave. They have got their liberty—so much good luck to have slavery partly destroyed; not entirely. I want it root and branch destroyed."

— SOJOURNER TRUTH

Who bids?
"INCENDIARY PICTURES."

By being A SLAVE
HIMSELF

"Although volume upon volume is written to prove slavery a very good thing, we never hear of the man who wished to take the good of it, by being a slave himself."
— ABRAHAM LINCOLN

ARGUING for slavery

"I will, in the name of humanity, which is outraged, in the name of liberty, which is fettered, in the name of the Constitution and the Bible, which are disregarded and trampled upon, dare to call into question and to denounce . . . slavery—the great sin and shame of America!"

— FREDERICK DOUGLASS

THE great sin and shame

The profits from the SLAVE TRADE

"The profits from the slave trade were part of the bedrock of our country's industrial development. Many people and institutions in every part of the country were complicit in the trans-Atlantic slave trade; and I have to say that this includes the Church of England."

— THOMAS BUTLER

It was THIS LABOUR

"... it was this [slave] labour that fed financial accumulation, economic expansion and the base for industrial acquisition, that is, the development of capitalism."

— STEPHEN SMALL

"In every man's mind the good seeds of liberty are planted, and he who brings his fellow down so low, as to make him contented with a condition of slavery, commits the highest crime against God and man."

— HENRY HIGHLAND GARNET

The highest crime against GOD and MAN

> "If you must bleed, let it all come at once—
> rather die freemen, than live to be slaves."
>
> — HENRY HIGHLAND GARNET

If you must BLEED

WRITTEN and sent on THE AIR

"Some of the most profound words ever uttered, some of the most beautiful thoughts ever contained in the hearts of men were written and sent on the air by black folk who were tied up in slavery."

— Reverend Benjamin L. Hooks

Most of us came here
IN CHAINS

"Most of us came here in chains and most of you came here to escape your chains. Your freedom was our slavery, and therein lies the bitter difference in the way we look at life."

— JOHN OLIVER KILLENS

"Your ancestors took the lash, the branding iron, humiliations, and oppression because one day they believed you would come along to flesh out the dream."

— Maya Angelou

You would flesh out
THE DREAM

America I AM
JUSTICE

After nearly two centuries of institutionalized slavery, Africans—both enslaved and free—began to collectively question what the words "all men are created equal" really meant in American society.

Enslaved Africans personified the imprint of democracy as they fought for freedom, not only for themselves but for their masters in the Revolutionary War. Some free blacks became soldiers fighting for the colonies in the hope that America would become a true democracy. But thousands of enslaved people ran away from their plantations and joined the British army.

Though the colonists prevailed, the failure to abolish slavery made the word "freedom" bitterly ironic for nearly one million black Americans. In this way, the American Revolution became the genesis for a black abolitionist revolution and the Civil War that would follow.

"And I hereby further declare all indented servants, Negroes, or others . . .
free, that are able and willing to bear arms, they joining His Majesty's Troops . . .
for the more speedily reducing the Colony to a proper sense of their duty,
to this Majesty's crown and dignity."

— Lord Dunmore's Proclamation

Brave Colored Artilleryman.

His MAJESTY'S TROOPS

The soil of every BATTLEFIELD

"[African American] blood is mingled with the soil of every battlefield, made glorious by revolutionary reminiscence, and [African American] bones have enriched the most productive lands of the country."

— ALEXANDER CRUMMELL

51

LIBERTY is DEAR

Peter Salem shoots Major Pitcairn at Bunker Hill.

"I served in the Revolution, in General Washington's army . . . Liberty is dear to my heart—I cannot endure the thought that my countrymen should be slaves."

— DR. HARRIS, A BLACK REVOLUTIONARY WAR VETERAN

"We have no property! we have no wives! we have no children! we have no city! no country! But we have a Father in heaven, and we are determined . . . to keep all his commandments; especially will we be obedient to our masters, so long as God . . . shall suffer us to be holden in bondage."

— PETITION OF SLAVES IN BOSTON IN 1773

We are DETERMINED

> "You used to be named Cornwallis, but it is Corn-wallis no longer; it must now be Cob-wallis, for General Washington has shelled off all the corn."

— AN AFRICAN AMERICAN SOLDIER AT THE BATTLE OF SARATOGA

Cornwallis NO LONGER

I LIKE my half

"Once, after Hull had accompanied his white employer to hear a 'distinguished mulatto preacher,' the man asked Hull, 'Well, how do you like nigger preaching?' to which Hull replied, 'Sir, he was half black and half white. I like my half, how did you like yours?'"

— AGRIPPA HULL

Christopher ATTUCKS

"A short distance from [Faneuil Hall] . . . where the disgusting rites of sacrificing a human being to slavery were lately performed, was the spot which was first moistened with American blood in *resisting slavery*, and among the first victims was a colored person."

— HON. CHARLES SUMNER

RESISTING slavery

"Although I have been servant to a Colonel forty years, my labors have not procured me any comfort. . . . With my poor daughter, I fear I shall pass the remainder of my days in slavery and misery. For her and myself, I beg freedom."

— A SLAVE NAMED BELINDA IN 1782

I beg FREEDOM

WE ARE to have SYMPATHY

"We are to have sympathy, but this, after all, is not to be confined to parties or colors, nor to towns or states, nor to a kingdom, but to the kingdoms of the whole earth, over whom Christ the King is head and grand master for all in distress."

— Prince Hall

MY Special PLACE

"I was a kind of bastard of the West . . . At the time I saw that
I had no other heritage which I could possibly hope to use . . .
I would have to appropriate those white centuries . . . I would
have to accept my special attitude, my special place in this scheme."

— PHILLIS WHEATLEY

"The world is a severe schoolmaster, for its frowns are less dangerous than its smiles and flatteries, and it is a difficult task to keep in the path of wisdom."

— PHILLIS WHEATLEY

Path of WISDOM

SHE WAS BORN a slave

Priceless CONTRIBUTION

"For to lay down one's life at the call of Duty is to lay down one's all. And this all of the general weighs no more than the all of a common soldier . . . When prince or beggar, master or slave, has given his life to a cause, he has given his utmost . . . Such was the priceless contribution which the poor, oppressed Negro made to American Independence."

— Archibald Grimké

America I AM
THE SOUL OF FREEDOM

By the 19th century, the socio-political imprint of the anti-slavery movement, led by African Americans like Frederick Douglass and others, continued to increase. It developed the Underground Railroad and the abolitionist movement became the world's first major interracial human rights movement. Despite slavery's existence, African American free communities in the North grew and thrived. Harriet Tubman, a conductor on the Underground Railroad who lived in the North at the time the Civil War began, worked as a scout and spy for the Union Army.

Black men fought heroically in the Civil War. In fact, so many African Americans enlisted that they made up one-fifth of all U.S. troops. And when Union soldiers marched into the South, enslaved people took advantage of the chaos of war to run away from plantations and find protection in the army camps.

Then, in 1863, over three centuries after the first arrival of enslaved Africans, President Abraham Lincoln issued the Emancipation Proclamation, and in 1865 the Civil War finally ended slavery.

The duty I OWE THE SLAVE

EMANCIPATION OF THE SLAVES.

"The duty I owe to the slave, to truth, and to God, demands that I should use my pen and tongue so long as life and health are vouchsafed to me to employ them or until the last chain shall fall from the limbs of the last slave in America and the world."

— WILLIAM WELLS BROWN

"The civil rights of a people being of the greatest value, it shall ever be our duty to vindicate our brethren when oppressed; and to lay the case before the publick."

— JOHN B. RUSSWURM AND SAMUEL CORNISH

THE CIVIL RIGHTS of a people

"There is not a man beneath the canopy of heaven
who does not know that slavery is wrong for him."

— FREDERICK DOUGLASS

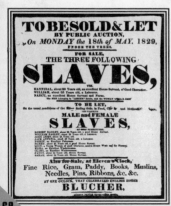

Slavery IS WRONG

"I had reasoned this out in my mind, there was one of two things I had a right to, liberty or death; if I could not have one, I would have the other."

— HARRIET TUBMAN

I never RAN MY TRAIN off the track

"I was the conductor of the Underground Railroad for eight years, and I can say what most conductors can't say; I never ran my train off the track and I never lost a passenger."

— HARRIET TUBMAN

"I freed a thousand slaves. I could have freed a thousand more if only they knew they were slaves."

— HARRIET TUBMAN

If only THEY KNEW
they were slaves

"Men talk of the Negro problem; there is no Negro problem. The problem is whether American people have loyalty enough, honor enough, patriotism enough to live up to their own Constitution."

— FREDERICK DOUGLASS

Frederick Douglass

THERE IS NO Negro problem

Creators of their DESTINY

"Every people should be the originators of their
own designs, the projector of their own schemes, and
creators of the events that lead to their destiny . . ."

— MARTIN ROBISON DELANY

My race needs NO SPECIAL DEFENSE

"My race needs no special defense, for the past history of them in this country proves them to be equal of any people anywhere. All they need is an equal chance in the battle of life."

— ROBERT SMALLS

"The color of the skin is in no way connected with the strength of the mind or intellectual powers."

— Preface to Banneker's Almanac, 1796

The COLOR of SKIN

"Power concedes nothing without a demand."

— FREDERICK DOUGLASS

POWER concedes nothing

"The recognition of our manhood throughout this land
is the abolition of slavery throughout the land."

— JAMES McCUNE SMITH

NO OTHER human power

MARTIN R. DELANEY, an author, physician, and leader before the Civil War

"Our elevation must be the result of self-efforts and work of our own hands. No other human power can accomplish it. If we but determine it shall be so, it will be so."

— MARTIN R. DELANY

"I was born a slave, but nature gave me a soul of a free man . . ."

— Toussaint Louverture

SOUL of a FREE MAN

"Once let the black man get upon his person the brass letters 'U.S.,' let him get an eagle on his button and a musket on his shoulder . . . and there is no power on earth which can deny that he has earned the right to citizenship."

— FREDERICK DOUGLASS

EARNED THE
right to citizenship

The destiny of the colored AMERICAN

"The destiny of the colored American, however this mighty
War shall terminate, is the destiny of America."

— FREDERICK DOUGLASS

If we hadn't
BECOME SOLDIERS

"If we hadn't become soldiers, all might have gone back as it was before."

— THOMAS LONG, CIVIL WAR SOLDIER

I gave my SERVICES WILLINGLY

> "However the Southern man may have been master of the negro, there were compensatory processes whereby certain negroes were masters of their masters' children."
> — JOHN S. WISE

MASTERS
of their masters' children

The cure for ALL ILLS

"The cure for all the ills and wrongs, the cares, the sorrows, and the crimes of humanity, all lie in that one word 'Love.' It is the divine vitality that everywhere produces and restores life."
— LYDIA M. CHILD

Enslave THE LIBERTY
of but ONE human being

"Enslave the liberty of but one human being
and the liberties of the world are put in peril."

— WILLIAM LLOYD GARRISON

"Brethren, arise, arise! Strike for your lives and liberties. Now is the day and the hour. Let every slave throughout the land do this and the days of slavery are numbered."

— HENRY HIGHLAND GARNET

Brethren, ARISE, ARISE!

America I AM
DENIED BUT NOT DEFEATED

After the Civil War, Congress moved quickly to dismantle the system of slavery and grant African Americans citizenship. The House and Senate adopted three amendments to the Constitution. The 13th Amendment abolished slavery throughout the United States. The 14th Amendment said that all persons born in the U.S. were citizens. This meant that African Americans could no longer legally be held as property. The 15th Amendment said that the right to vote belonged to all citizens. Numerous black men were elected to Congress. For a time, African Americans enjoyed full citizenship rights.

Yet these short-lived achievements were stripped away by the "Black Codes" that undermined the voting and educational rights, and economic opportunities that African Americans had briefly experienced.

THE Negro question

The **IDEA** that has **MOVED ME**

"I want you to understand that I respect the rights of the poorest and weakest of colored people, oppressed by the slave system, just as much as I do those of the most wealthy and powerful. That is the idea that has moved me, and that alone."

— JOHN BROWN

Violation of
SELF-EVIDENT TRUTHS

"Slavery, throughout its entire existence in the United States is none other than a most barbarous, unprovoked, and unjustifiable War of one portion of its citizens upon another portion . . . in utter disregard and violation of those eternal and self-evident truths set forth in our Declaration of Independence."

— JOHN BROWN

"There has been houses broken open, windows smashed and doors broken down in the dead hours of the night. . . . Men have been knocked down and unmercifully beaten and yet the authorities do not notice it at all. We would open a school here, but are almost afraid to do so, not knowing that we have any protection for life or limb."

— AFRICAN AMERICAN CITIZENS OF CALHOUN, GEORGIA

Authorities do not NOTICE

"Ole missus used tu read de good book tu us, black 'uns, on Sunday evenin's, but she mostly read dem places whar it says, 'Sarvints obey your masters,' an' didn't stop tu splane it like de teachers; an' now we is free, dar's heaps o' tings in dat ole book, we is jes sufferin' tu larn."

— AN ELDERLY BLACK MAN IN MISSISSIPPI IN 1869

WE IS jes sufferin' tu larn

They can't LEARN

"I do assure you, you might as well try to teach your horse or mule to read, as to teach these niggers. They can't learn. Some of [the house servants and urban blacks] were smart enough for anything. But the country niggers are like monkeys. You can't learn them to come in when it rains."

— A WHITE WOMAN, ADVISING A TEACHER FOR THE FREEDMEN'S BUREAU

Conscientious MEN

"I know this single word, 'duty,' carries with it all that need be addressed to right-thinking, right-feeling, and conscientious men."

— ROBERT BROWN ELLICOTT, U.S. REPRESENTATIVE, 1871–1874

"If [an African American] is a man, he is entitled to all the rights and privileges of any other man. There can be no grades of citizenship under the American flag."

— John Adams Hyman, U.S. Representative, 1875–1877

No grades of CITIZENSHIP

"We [black Americans] are earnest in our support of the Government. We are earnest in the house of the nation's perils and dangers; and now, in our country's comparative peace and tranquility, we are earnest for our rights."

— REPRESENTATIVE JOSEPH HAYNE RAINEY

THE nation's perils

Everything CONNECTED

"When the election was held everything connected with it was quiet and peaceable and I [was] elected by a large majority [January 20, 1870] . . . While there I did all I could for the benefit of my needed and much imposed upon people."

— HIRAM RHODES REVELS,
THE FIRST AFRICAN AMERICAN SENATOR IN THE U.S.

Its own MERITS

"I appear here more to acknowledge this high privilege than to
make an argument before this House. . . . I do not expect, nor do
I ask, that there shall be any favor shown me on account of my race . . .
I wish the case to be decided on its own merits and nothing else."

— JOHN WILLIS MENARD

"Be mild with the mild, shrewd with the crafty, confiding to the honest, rough to the ruffian, and a thunderbolt to the liar. But in all this, never be unmindful of your own dignity."

— JOHN BROWN

Be mild with the mild,

SHREWD WITH THE CRAFTY

America I AM
INVINCIBLE

Reconstruction ended when President Hayes made a backroom deal with Southern politicians. He withdrew federal troops from the South and allowed Southern states to take control. These states began passing Jim Crow laws, which were enforced by terrorist groups like the Ku Klux Klan. Black people were coerced back into a slavery-like position in Southern society and suffered from racism in the North, too. Other minorities were also oppressed. Despite the Civil War, America still had not achieved full democracy.

But all these negatives were met with positive—and now more vocally forceful—African American resistance. Such prohibitions led to the establishment of pioneering civil rights organizations like the NAACP, the Urban League, the National Council of Negro Women, and the Universal Negro Improvement Association.

Ironically, the Jim Crow period created one of the greatest eras in African American cultural creativity.

"De big bee suck de blossom, /
De little bee makes honey, /
De black man makes de cotton and corn, /
And de white man totes de money."

— SONG SUNG BY BLACK FIELD HANDS IN THE JIM CROW SOUTH

De white man TOTES DE MONEY

"[I]f you don't make enough to have some left you ain't done nothin, except given the other fellow your labor. That crop out there goin' to prosper enough for him to get his and get what I owe him; he's making his profit but he ain't going to let me rise . . . what am I g'tting for my labor? I ain't g'ttin'."

— NED COBB, A BLACK ALABAMA SHARECROPPER

Is it POSSIBLE, and PROBABLE

"Is it possible, and probable, that nine millions of men can make effective progress in economic lines if they are deprived of political rights, made a servile caste, and allowed only the most meager chance for developing their exceptional men? If history and reason give any distinct answer to these questions, it is an emphatic No."

— W. E. B. Du Bois

> "The nineteenth-century lynching mob cuts off ears, toes, and fingers, strips off flesh, and distributes portions of the body as souvenirs among the crowd."
>
> — Ida B. Wells-Barnett

SOUVENIRS among the CROWD

"I felt that one better die fighting against injustice than to die like a dog or a rat in a trap. I had already determined to sell my life as dearly as possible if attacked. I felt if I could take one lyncher with me, this would even up the score a bit."

— IDA B. WELLS-BARNETT

UNITED STATES ATROCITIES.

LYNCH LAW

BY

Ida B. Wells.

With an Introduction by S. J. Celestine Edwards.

Price Sixpence.

LONDON:
"LUX" NEWSPAPER AND PUBLISHING COMPANY, LIMITED,
18, PATERNOSTER ROW, E.C.

DIE
fighting against injustice

Die a natural DEATH

"In this perilous world, if a black boy wanted to live a halfway normal life and die a natural death he had to learn early the art of how to get along with white folks."

— BENJAMIN MAYS

109

DON'T CHALLENGE
white people

"You pass white people on your way, you get off the sidewalk.
Give them the sidewalk. Don't challenge white people."

— CHARLES GRATTON

"The people must know before they can act,
and there is no educator to compare with the press."

— IDA B. WELLS-BARNETT

The people MUST KNOW

"For I am my mother's daughter, and the drums of Africa still beat in my heart. They will not let me rest while there's a single Negro boy or girl without a chance to prove his worth."

— MARY MCLEOD BETHUNE

a CHANCE
to prove HIS WORTH

Mystery of THE UNIVERSE

"When I was young, I said to God, 'God, tell me the mystery of the universe.' But God answered, 'That knowledge is for me alone.' So I said, 'God, tell me the mystery of the peanut.' Then God said, 'Well George that's more nearly your size.' And he told me."

— George Washington Carver

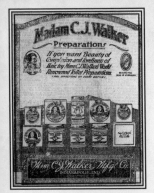

Don't wait for
OPPORTUNITIES

"I had to make my own living and my own opportunity . . . Don't sit down and wait for the opportunities to come; you have to get up and make them."

— MADAM C.J. WALKER

"If we accept and acquiesce in the face of discrimination, we accept the responsibility ourselves and allow those responsible to salve their conscience by believing that they have our acceptance and concurrence. We should, therefore, protest openly everything . . . that smacks of discrimination or slander."

— MARY McLEOD BETHUNE

PROTEST openly EVERYTHING

"My grandfather was a branded slave. The letter P, nine inches high, was burned into his back. I stood on a chair at the age of ten and traced down his brown back with my finger that P of seared human flesh. I swore to my God that I would not rest until I had wiped that brand from my memory and from the conscience of white America."

— ADAM CLAYTON POWELL, JR.

I swore to GOD

Promotion of EQUALITY

"Promotion of Equality: Any person . . . who shall be guilty of printing, publishing or circulating printed, typewritten or written matter urging or presenting for public acceptance or general information, arguments or suggestions in favor of social equality or of intermarriage between whites and negroes, shall be guilty of a misdemeanor and subject to fine or imprisonment."

— MARTIN LUTHER KING, JR.,
NATIONAL HISTORIC SITE INTERPRETIVE STAFF, MISSISSIPPI

THE LAW IS not executed

"A colored man cannot get any charge made against a white man here . . . They take the colored man and send him to the penitentiary and the law is not executed on the white man at all. We well have to have some protection or else go away from here."

— JANE AND MINNIE EVANS

"The hate and scorn showered on us Negro officers by our fellow Americans convinced me that there was not sense in my dying for a world ruled by them. I made up my mind that if I got through this war I would study law and use my time fighting for men who could not strike back."

— CHARLES HAMILTON HOUSTON

Men who could not STRIKE BACK

"And thus goes segregation which is the most far-reaching
development in history of the Negro since the enslavement of the race."

— CARTER G. WOODSON

. . . SEGREGATION . . .
the enslavement OF THE RACE

"As a matter of history, the Fourteenth Amendment was not understood to ban segregation on the basis of race."

— CASS SUNSTEIN

SIMPLY not welcome

"During the days of segregation, there was not a place of higher learning for African Americans. They were simply not welcome in many of the traditional schools and from this backward policy grew the network of historical black colleges and universities."

— MICHAEL N. CASTLE

> "At the bottom of education, at the bottom of politics, even at the bottom of religion there must be for our race economic independence."
>
> — BOOKER T. WASHINGTON

Economic INDEPENDENCE

"I have learned that success is to be measured not so much by the position that one has reached in life as by the obstacles which he has had to overcome while trying to succeed."

— BOOKER T. WASHINGTON

Obstacles OVERCOME

Drama of FRUSTRATION

"The players in this drama of frustration and indignity are not commas or semicolons in a legislative thesis; they are people, human beings, citizens of the United States of America."

— Roy Wilkins

FIGHTING FOR education

"Nothing should be overlooked in fighting for better education.
Be persistent and ornery: this will be good for the lethargic educational
establishment and will aid the whole cause of public education."

— ROY WILKINS

"We conclude that in the field of public education, the doctrine of 'separate but equal' has no place. Separate educational facilities are inherently unequal."

— THE SUPREME COURT, BROWN V. BOARD OF EDUCATION, 1955

Separate but EQUAL
has NO PLACE

America I AM
SPIRIT

Church has always been central to the black community. The anti-slavery movement was rooted in religion—from the founding of the first black church in 1792 and the first black denomination, the African Methodist Episcopal, in 1794. Later, as black people moved out of the rural South, urban churches formed the heart of their new neighborhoods.

Historically, black churches also advanced critical secular and cultural change. For some, black Christians were the embodiment of "turning the other cheek," because they kept the faith despite enslavement or second-class citizenship. Churches helped build the Underground Railroad, and ministers became leaders in the ongoing struggle for equality. Culturally, the black church preserved a distinctive black preaching style, and gave us gospel music, which influenced rhythm and blues, soul, and other musical forms. The civil rights movement was born in the black church, led by the incomparable Baptist minister, Dr. Martin Luther King, Jr.

"... nothing is stable; all things are changeable. Let us seek those things which are sure and steadfast, and let us pray God that, while we remain here, he would give us the grace of patience, and strength to bear up under all our troubles ..."

— Prince Hall

STRENGTH to bear up

Gospel is FREE

"This land, which we have watered with our tears and our blood, is now our mother country, and we are well satisfied to stay where wisdom abounds and gospel is free."

— RICHARD ALLEN

Religion without
HUMANITY

"Religion without humanity is very poor human stuff."

— SOJOURNER TRUTH

"I will not let prejudice or any of its attendant humiliations and injustices bear me down to spiritual defeat."

— James Weldon Johnson

> "If we are going to pray for liberation and equality,
> then we also have to work for it."
>
> — LEONTINE T.C. KELLY

LIBERATION and equality

The soul of the race MADE MANIFEST

"These songs are to Negro culture what the works of the great poets are to English culture: They are the soul of the race made manifest."

— PAUL ROBESON

There is no language that
GOD DOES NOT UNDERSTAND

"Every man prays in his own language and
there is no language that God does not understand."

— DUKE ELLINGTON

"My goal is to live the truly religious life and express it in my music."

— JOHN COLTRANE

Express it in my MUSIC

"God has created his people to be perfect, whole and complete, and filled and surrounded in and with prosperity. Prosperity does not just mean money; it means health, joy and peace and all the good things that God is."

— REVEREND DR. JOHNNIE COLEMAN

ALL good things

"Love, then, is not an emotion. It is deeper than that. It's the embodiment of principles that bring joy and peace to human beings: Freedom, justice, equality, obedience to The Will of God. God is the embodiment of all righteous principles . . ."

— MINISTER LOUIS FARRAKHAN

Teach us
THY FORGIVENESS

"We turn to thee, our Father, with the great hunger for wholeness and cleanliness that before our own eyes, even as before thee, we shall not be ashamed. Teach us thy forgiveness that we may learn, our Father, how to forgive ourselves. Oh God, God, God. Teach us while there is still time."

— HOWARD THURMAN

> "Don't ask what the world needs. Ask what makes you come alive, and go do it. Because what the world needs is people who have come alive."
>
> — HOWARD THURMAN

What makes YOU COME ALIVE

"God is as dependent on you as you are on Him."

— MAHALIA JACKSON

GOD is as dependent

GOD
is inside
YOU

"God is inside you and inside everybody else. But only them that search for it inside find it. And sometimes it just manifest itself even if you are not looking, or don't know what you looking for."

— ALICE WALKER

Out of the CHURCH

"The most segregated hour is the hour of worship. The civil rights movement came out of the church. I believe that God is trying to get all of his children at one table."

— ALFONZO SURRETT

"If you are neutral in situations of injustice, you have chosen the side of the oppressor. If an elephant has its foot on the tail of a mouse and you say that you are neutral, the mouse will not appreciate your neutrality."

— BISHOP DESMOND TUTU

CHOOSING sides

"There are some fires you can't get out of—you've got to go through the fire—you've got to go through the flood—you've got to go through the test—you've got to go through the struggle that you might decrease and he might increase."

— T.D. JAKES

You've got to go
THROUGH THE FIRE

STRUGGLE for America's moral CENTER

"We're in a struggle for the soul of this country . . . We're in
a struggle for America's moral center. And unless that can be
made straight, I'm not too sure any of the other battles are winnable."

— HARRY BELAFONTE

America I AM
PATRIOTIC

African Americans have fought in every American war and, until the mid-20th century, they fought in a segregated military in which they were not treated equally. During World War I, the U.S. denied the Medal of Honor to its deserving black soldiers, but France gave its highest military honor, the *Croix de Guerre,* to the entire 369th Infantry—the "Harlem Hellfighters"—for its bravery in combat. Unfortunately, the black heroes of World War I came home to a segregated country where they were still second-class citizens.

When World War II began, people in the black community remembered the outcomes of World War I. They did not want their young men and women to fight another war for democracy and again come home to a racist nation. Black newspapers across the country mounted a "Double V" campaign—for victory overseas and victory over segregation at home. Though segregation continued, some were able to get better jobs. Black women were able to become nurses and WACs, and a small number of black men became fighter pilots—the famous Tuskegee Airmen.

Shortly after World War II, President Harry Truman ordered the integration of the U.S. military. While blacks had achieved institutional equality, the Vietnam War draft raised questions about equality in practice. Many civil rights leaders were also figures in the antiwar movement. Nevertheless, African American soldiers served with distinction during the conflict, and continue to serve today.

"Many have been tremendously tested. You have suffered hardships and many privations. Your record has sent a thrill of joy and satisfaction to the hearts of millions of black and white Americans . . . I hope no one will do anything in peace to spoil the magnificent record your troops have made in war."

— ROBERT RUSSA MOTON, TUSKEGEE INSTITUTE

TREMENDOUSLY tested

Sometimes we did a little MORE

"No one group of people made this country great; that everybody had to contribute in some way; and the 369th Harlem Hellfighters did their part the same as others. And sometimes we did a little more than others."

— Major General Nathaniel James

PROVE our WORTH

"We would go through any ordeal that came our way,
be it in garrison existence or combat, to prove our worth."

— GENERAL BENJAMIN O. DAVIS, JR

"We colored Americans adopt the double VV for a double victory. The first V for victory over our enemies from without, the second V for victory over our enemies from within."

— Serviceman James G. Thompson

Double VICTORY

"I've fought in three wars and three more wouldn't be too many to defend my country. I love America and as she has weaknesses or ills, I'll hold her hand."

— GENERAL DANIEL "CHAPPIE" JAMES, JR.

I love AMERICA

"The atmosphere of the whole country was to
get in the service and help. I wanted to do my part."

— WILLIAM McBURNEY

SEALED, not healed

"The wounds of Black World War II soldiers
have been sealed, not healed, by . . . history."

— FRANK J. TOLLAND

No colors, NO BOUNDARIES

"Now, you're not supposed to be so blind with patriotism
that you can't face reality. Wrong is wrong, no matter who says it . . ."

— Malcolm X

Blind with PATRIOTISM

THEY RECEIVED NOTHING

"African-Americans had answered the country's every call from its infancy . . . Yet, the fame and fortune that were their just due never came. For their blood spent, lives lost, and battles won, they received nothing. They went back to slavery, real or economic, consigned there by hate, prejudice, bigotry, and intolerance."

— GENERAL COLIN POWELL

True PATRIOTISM

"I think that true patriotism is expressed by those who live it so much that they will not leave it alone until it lives up to its noble precepts and keeps its lofty promises and commitments to be the land of the free as well as the home of the brave."

— THE REVEREND JOSEPH LOWERY

"They were just like me and just like you. These guys were warfighters for our nation. They did their job, not with the intent to make a name for black aviators, but to be fighters for their country."

— CAPTAIN GLENN GONZALES SPEAKING OF THE TUSKEGEE AIRMEN

Black AVIATORS

"I'm looking to be shot any time I step out of my car . . . If I die, it will be in a good cause. I've been fighting for America just as much as the soldiers in Vietnam."

— MEDGAR EVERS

Fighting for AMERICA

PROUD for having SERVED

"Even after 31 years, I'm still caught up in the Vietnam war . . .
It is still very real for me. And although I want to feel proud for
having served my country, I think it is important for all Americans
who see themselves reflected in that stone to remember the
War honestly. We owe that to ourselves and to our children."

— GLENN L. BAKER

America I AM
CONSCIENCE

The advent of the civil rights movement fostered landmark milestones in American history, and would once again show the African American gift to democracy, including legal, law enforcement, legislative, and electoral imprints. In December 1955, Rosa Parks took the first step in the modern civil rights movement by refusing to give up her seat in the white section of a segregated bus: the Montgomery Bus Boycott began, advanced by Dr. Martin Luther King, and following the nonviolent teachings of Mahatma Gandhi.

The NAACP began to challenge segregation laws in court. Courageous individuals participated in boycotts, marches, voter registration drives, and freedom rides. Black men and women led the movement, but were joined by people of all races, religions, ethnic groups, and nationalities. Protesters were met with violence, but their struggle began a wave of change that continues today. The civil rights movement would become a model for other freedom movements around the world.

> "There is a higher law than the law of government.
> That's the law of conscience."
>
> — STOKELY CARMICHAEL

The LAW of conscience

Dignity and SELF-RESPECT

"... I was a person with dignity and self-respect, and I should not set my sights lower than anybody else just because I was black."

— ROSA PARKS

The right to STAND TALL

"The Civil Rights Movement that rearranged the social order of this country
did not emanate from the halls of the Harvards and the Princetons and Cornells.
It came from simple, unlettered people who learned that they had the right
to stand tall and that nobody can ride a back that isn't bent."

— DOROTHY COTTON

"Nonviolence is a powerful and just weapon. It is a weapon unique in history, which cuts without wounding, and ennobles the man who wields it. It is a sword that heals."

— MARTIN LUTHER KING, JR.

NONVIOLENCE . . .
A SWORD that heals

"Black people have begged, prayed, petitioned and demonstrated, among other things, to get the racist power structure of America to right the wrongs which have historically been perpetrated against Black people . . . A people who have suffered so much for so long at the hands of a racist society must draw the line somewhere."

— HUEY P. NEWTON

TO RIGHT the wrongs

Protest confers DIGNITY

"When an individual is protesting society's refusal
to acknowledge his dignity as a human being,
his very act of protest confers dignity on him."

— BAYARD RUSTIN

I saw DEATH

"I thought I was going to die a few times. On the Freedom Ride in the year 1961, when I was beaten at the Greyhound bus station in Montgomery, I thought I was going to die. On March 7th, 1965, when I was hit in the head with a night stick by a state trooper at the foot of the Edmund Pettus Bridge, I thought I was going to die. I thought I saw death, but nothing can make me question the philosophy of nonviolence."

— JOHN LEWIS

COURAGE
in spite of FEAR

"Not only had we come from Selma to Montgomery—a distance of more than fifty miles—but we had come from the outer regions of second-class citizenship to the threshold of full participation in American democracy."

— RALPH ABERNATHY

Selma to
MONTGOMERY

Little Rock was that SPARK

"Events in history occur when the time has ripened for them, but they need a spark. Little Rock was that spark at that stage of the struggle of the American Negro for justice."

— DAISY BATES

A SYMPHONY of protest

"The Civil Rights Movement was a symphony of protest."

— QUINCY JONES

"There is never time in the future in which we will work out our salvation. The challenge is in the moment, the time is always now."

— James Baldwin

The time is ALWAYS NOW

"In order for us as poor and oppressed people to become part of a society that is meaningful, the system under which we now exist has to be radically changed . . . It means facing a system that does not lend itself to your needs and devising means by which you change that system."

— ELLA BAKER

CHANGE
that system

I own a SHARE

"This is my country. I own a share in it. I have a vested interest in it. My ancestors helped create it . . . build it . . . make it strong and great, and rich. All of this belongs to me as much as it belongs to any American with a white skin."

— RALPH BUNCHE

Struggle to
RESPOND WITH DECENCY

"Children holding hands, walking with the wind. That is America
to me—not just the movement for civil rights but the endless
struggle to respond with decency, dignity and a sense of brotherhood
to all the challenges that face us as a nation, as a whole."

— JOHN LEWIS

"Racism, war, and poverty were heavy burdens;
to challenge injustice was an easy burden."

— ANDREW YOUNG

TO CHALLENGE injustice

"It takes a person with a stout heart and great courage and uncompromising honesty to look the history of this country squarely in the face and tell it like it is."

— JOHN HOPE FRANKLIN

Uncompromising HONESTY

TELL the truth TODAY

"Sometimes it seems like to tell the truth today is to run the risk of being killed. But if I fall, I'll fall five feet four inches forward in the fight for freedom."

— FANNIE LOU HAMER

FIGHTING racism

"If you believe in fighting racism, you make a commitment for the rest of your life. There's no getting off that train. You can't say, 'I've put five years in fighting racism and now I am finished.' No, you are not finished. Our job is to fight it every day, to continue to shove it down and when it rises up to shove it down even harder."

— REPRESENTATIVE PARREN JAMES MITCHELL

"... I was not included in that 'We the People.' I felt somehow for years that George Washington and Alexander Hamilton just left me out by mistake. But through the process of amendment, interpretation, and court decision, I have finally been included in 'We the People.' My faith in the Constitution is whole; it is complete, it is total."

— CONGRESSWOMAN BARBARA JORDAN

MY FAITH in the CONSTITUTION

"For any of you who would linger in the cemetery and tarry around the grave, I have news for you. We have business on the road to freedom . . . We must prove to white America that **you can kill the leader** but you cannot kill the dream."

— RALPH D. ABERNATHY

YOU CAN
kill the leader

"Visionary leadership is based on a leap of faith and a labor of love."

— Cornel West

America I AM
CULTURE

Throughout history, African Americans used the gift of story and song to create an indelible imprint. Black musicians invented gospel, blues, ragtime, jazz, soul, rhythm and blues, rock 'n' roll, and hip hop, forms that have shaped the conception of modern music the world over. Black entertainers like Sydney Poitier, Harry Belafonte, Bill Cosby, Denzel Washington, Ruby Dee, Halle Berry, and Morgan Freeman have helped define Broadway, film, and television. The contributions of writers such as Richard Wright, Langston Hughes, Zora Neale Hurston, James Baldwin, Alice Walker, and Toni Morrison have helped shape not just American letters, but the entire Western literary canon. In the world of sports, black men and women were once outside the mainstream; now they are national icons. From Jesse Owens to Joe Louis, from Wilma Rudolph to Muhammad Ali, and from Arthur Ashe to Venus and Serena Williams—these incomparable figures have raised the level of excellence for all in the American cultural landscape.

> "A people may become great through many means, but there is only one measure by which its greatness is recognized and acknowledged. The final measure of the greatness of all peoples is the amount and standard of the literature and art they have produced."

> — James Weldon Johnson

THE FINAL MEASURE
of the greatness

Important that my work
BE AFRICAN-AMERICAN

"It's very important to me that my work be African-American; if it assimilates into a different or larger pool, so much the better."

— TONI MORRISON

LEGACIES of the AFRICAN PAST

"Music, dance, religion do not have artifacts as their end products . . .
the most important legacies of the African past, even to the contemporary
black American blues, jazz, and the adaptation of the Christian religion,
all rely heavily on African culture."

— AMIRI BARAKA

"I recognize no American culture which is not the partial creation of Black people. I recognize no American style in literature, in dance, in music, even in assembly-line processes, which does not bear the mark of the American Negro."

— RALPH ELLISON

BEAR THE MARK
of the AMERICAN NEGRO

"True black writers speak as blacks, about blacks, to blacks."

— GWENDOLYN BROOKS

TRUE BLACK writers

ART because it's TRUTHFUL

"I like to think that if truth has any bearing on art, my poetry and prose is art because it's truthful."

— NIKKI GIOVANNI

195

It's like **POETRY**

"Musicians give you insight into the feeling—
it's like poetry—of the time they lived in . . ."

— MAX ROACH

"Blues is the best literature that we Blacks have. It's very articulate."

— AUGUST WILSON

BLUES IS the best literature

"Everybody loves them . . . in whatever country, it doesn't matter what the native tongue of my audience is, they've heard the spirituals before, and they want to hear them again, and they want to hear them out of a black mouth."

— JESSYE NORMAN

They've HEARD THE SPIRITUALS before

The people treated us LIKE KINGS

"In those same towns where we couldn't get a hotel room or a meal in a decent restaurant—even if we could pay for it— the people treated us like kings once we got up on the stage."

— LIONEL HAMPTON

Every child must be given
AN OPPORTUNITY

"Dance Theatre of Harlem broke down barriers and perceptions and ideologies of what people can or cannot do and that every child must be given an opportunity, which is really a major part of the American Dream."

— ARTHUR MITCHELL

"My job is to be resilient. That's why I call life a dance."

— BILL T. JONES

Be RESILIENT

> "Never before have so many white Americans paid
> Black Americans that sincerest form of flattery—imitation."
>
> — JOHN H. JOHNSON

Sincerest form of
FLATTERY—IMITATION

Culturally in TUNE

"I will maintain a home that is culturally in tune with the best of African-American history, struggle and future."
— HAKI R. MADHUBUTI

America I AM
WORLD

Since setting foot on American soil nearly 500 years ago, African Americans have faced great adversity yet still achieved extraordinary accomplishments. The black economic imprint—once generating wealth solely for slaveowners now generates wealth for stockholders through such African American business titans as Kenneth Chenault and Oprah Winfrey. The socio-political imprint was manifested in the black abolitionist movement, the African American challenge to the Democratic Party's support of Jim Crow, the modern civil rights movement, and has produced Barack Obama, America's first African American president. The spiritual imprint began with enslaved African Americans secretly having church in the woods and has culminated in the growth of social justice ministries and pastors such as Bishop T.D. Jakes preaching in his unique African style to megachurch congregations. The cultural imprint originated with the preservation of the African griot tradition of storytelling that transcended the barriers of a separate and unequal educational system to produce the genius of Toni Morrison, winner of the Nobel Prize in Literature. The African musical traditions of call and response and polyrhythmic structure brought to the New World have served as a foundation for American musical innovation and have influenced nearly every modern musical form.

Thanks to these priceless contributions, today we celebrate the incomparable African American Imprint around the world.

"To be free—to walk the good American earth as equal citizens, to live without fear, to enjoy the fruits of our toil, to give our children every opportunity in life—that dream which we have held so long in our hearts is today the destiny that we hold in our hands."

— PAUL ROBESON

THE DESTINY
that we hold in our hands

On the FIRING LINE

"I want to be out there on the firing line, helping, directing or doing
something to try to make this a better world, a better place to live."

— JOHN HOPE FRANKLIN

Education with
MAXIMUM EFFORT

"We cannot afford to settle for being just average; we must learn as much as we can to be the best that we can. The key word is education—that knowledge—education with maximum effort. Without it, we cannot be in charge of ourselves or anyone else."

— BILL COSBY

"Hearts are the strongest when they beat in response to noble ideals."

— RALPH BUNCHE

NOBLE Ideals

"The fact that we're different colors is basically just an excuse . . . But if people **understand the differences** a little better, to blend the colors, which was my job as a comedian, it's possible to see we're all the same."

— Richard Pryor

UNDERSTAND
the differences

Take a small piece of this HUGE THING

"I say that if each person in this world will simply take a small piece of this huge thing, this tablecloth, bedspread, whatever, and work it regardless of the color of the yarn, we will have harmony on this planet."

— CICELY TYSON

ROOT FOR
somebody else's FREEDOM

"You can only appreciate freedom when you finally find yourself in a position where you're rooting for somebody else's freedom, and not worried about your own."

— RUBY DEE

> "In recognizing the humanity of our fellow beings,
> we pay ourselves the highest tribute."
>
> — THURGOOD MARSHALL

Recognize THE HUMANITY

"Of course, being a black boxing champ is nothing new. There have been many great boxing champions of color, Joe Louis being one of the greatest . . . and all of us have been fighting for the same thing—progress."

— JOE FRAZIER

FIGHTING
for the same thing

"I loved Muhammad Ali. I loved what he stood for. He even went to jail for his belief. [And I think] . . . that's the ultimate role model . . . I don't always say what's on my mind, but I do stand up for what I believe in."

— SERENA WILLIAMS

It takes CHARACTER

"Ability may get you to the top,
but it takes character to keep you there."

— STEVIE WONDER

"Never let your head hang down. **Never give up and sit and grieve.** Find another way. And don't pray when it rains if you don't pray when the sun shines."

— SATCHEL PAIGE

NEVER GIVE UP and sit and grieve

"You have to **believe in yourself** when no one else does—
that makes you a winner right there."

— VENUS WILLIAMS

Believe in YOURSELF

"A life is not important except in the impact it has on other lives."

— JACKIE ROBINSON

219

The evolution OF THE RACE

"Our ancestors were required to die as part of the evolution of the race.
They died in order that our genius could be spread throughout the world."

— Iyanla Vanzant

> "Life stretches in front of and behind us,
> made up of the actions we and others took."
>
> — MAE C. JEMISON

Made up of THE ACTIONS

"It's the journey that matters. Learning is more important than the test. Practice well, and the games will take care of themselves, whether you've been kicked in the teeth or life just couldn't get any sweeter, it keeps rolling on . . . and then there's another game."

— TONY DUNGY

LEARNING IS
more important than THE TEST

It's HOW YOU RUN that MARATHON

"Life is no sprint. It's a marathon—a long, long, long-distance
race over hills and through valleys, sometimes even with
stops along the way, and it's how you run that marathon,
not how soon you get to the finish line, that matters."

— JESSE OWENS

All are equal, all are free,
AND ALL DESERVE A CHANCE

"The time has come to reaffirm our enduring spirit; to choose our better history; to carry forward that precious gift, that noble idea, passed on from generation to generation: The God-given promise that all are equal, all are free, and all deserve a chance to pursue their full measure of happiness."

— BARACK OBAMA

"I believe in God who made of one blood all nations that on earth do dwell. I believe that all men, black and brown and white, are brothers, varying through time and opportunity, in form and gift and feature, but differing in no essential particular, and alike in soul and the possibility of infinite development."

— W. E. B. Du Bois

Possibility of
INFINITE DEVELOPMENT

ACKNOWLEDGMENTS

Editor Clarence V. Reynolds

I am grateful for the heroic and inspiring spirits and voices who left these treasured words of encouragement for us to share. And I owe a deep, heartfelt thanks to my loving parents, supportive family, and friends.

oOo

The SmileyBooks Editors

Creating the America I AM *Journal* has been an incredible education and labor of love. It is a privilege to be able to pass on this accumulated wisdom and history, and we hope it provides a new inspiring space for rewarding personal reflection.

We are grateful to Tavis Smiley for mounting the award-winning America I AM exhibit, the inspiration for this journal. His vision and dedication to sharing this rich tapestry of history with people from coast to coast is truly awe-inspiring.

SmileyBooks Editorial Board member Denise Pines served as our personal America I AM Encyclopedia. Her vital and generous feedback ensured that the heart of the exhibit would beat on every page.

Our humblest thanks to Cheryl Woodruff, SmileyBooks President and the *Journal*'s creative *auteur*. Her tireless guidance, encouragement, and astute aesthetic sensitivity kept us on track and made this project a true pleasure to work on.

Editor Clarence Reynolds's enthusiasm was contagious, and his eagerness to reach and teach others through our portable AIA *Journal* inspired us all. We are indebted for his many contributions.

This project could not have been completed without the untiring and dauntless SmileyBooks editorial team, especially John McWilliams, whose keen editorial eye, commitment to excellence, and unfailing support was essential to this project's completion. We are likewise grateful for Kirsten Melvey's assiduous quotation research and Colby Hamilton's detective-like photo research. Their efforts constitute much of the *Journal*'s behind-the-scenes magic.

A very special thanks to Diane Allford, who provided additional photo research and generous support.

A heartfelt thank you to LeRoy Henderson, whose exceptional photography brought the modern era in the *Journal* to life.

This journal would not have been completed nearly as well without the invaluable support and guidance of our Hay House design team, Charles McStravick and Jami Goddess. Jami's beautiful design and extraordinary commitment elevated this project to new heights. We are deeply grateful.

PHOTO CREDITS

Images on the following pages courtesy of the University of Massachusetts Amherst, W. E. B. Du Bois Papers, MS 312, Special Collections and University Archives, W. E. B. Du Bois Library: facing page 1, 4, 6, 8, 10, 12, 14.

Images on the following pages courtesy of the Library of Congress: 2, 16, 28, 30, 40, 42, 54, 58, 60, 64, 66, 70, 74, 82, 86, 94, 96, 98, 100, 104,106, 110, 112, 114, 118, 122, 124, 128, 132, 136, 138, 148, 150, 152, 158, 160, 168, 172, 174, 176.

Images on the following pages courtesy of the New York Public Library: 18, 20, 22, 24, 26, 32, 34, 38, 44, 46, 48, 50, 52, 56, 68, 72, 76, 78, 80, 88, 90, 92, 108, 120, 130.

Images on the following pages courtesy of LeRoy Henderson: 128, 134, 140, 142, 144, 146, 164, 166, 170, 178, 180, 182, 184, 186, 188, 190, 192, 196, 198, 200, 202, 204, 206, 208, 210, 212, 214, 216, 218, 220, 222, 224.

Image on page 62 courtesy of Bridgeman Art Library New York.

Image on page 84 courtesy of the National Park Service, Timucuan Ecological & Historical Preserve, TIMU 3112.

Images on pages 102 and 154 courtesy of the Associated Press.

Original illustrations on the following pages by Shepard Fairey: 9,13, 15, 117, 145, 147, 169, 171, 173, 177, 183, 199, 207, 219, 221.

Original illustrations on the following pages by Jami Goddess: 39, 47, 51, 55, 57, 63, 73, 77, 81, 83, 85, 87, 91, 97, 99, 105, 109, 113, 115, 125, 127, 135, 137, 151, 155, 157, 159, 161, 163, 175, 179, 181, 187, 193, 195, 197, 201, 203, 215, 217, 223, 225.

ABOUT THE EDITOR

Clarence V. Reynolds is an independent journalist and editor. He has worked for numerous publications, including *The Network Journal, Black Issues Book Review, Discover, and B. Smith with Style.* He lives in New York City.

We hope you enjoyed this SMILEYBOOKS publication.
If you would like to receive additional information, please contact:

SMILEYBOOKS

Distributed by:

Hay House, Inc.
P.O. Box 5100
Carlsbad, CA 92018-5100

(760) 431-7695 or **(800) 654-5126**
(760) 431-6948 (fax) or **(800) 650-5115 (fax)**
www.hayhouse.com® • **www.hayfoundation.org**

oOo

Published and distributed in Australia by: Hay House Australia Pty. Ltd.
18/36 Ralph St. • Alexandria NSW 2015 • Phone: 612-9669-4299
Fax: 612-9669-4144 • www.hayhouse.com.au

Published and distributed in the United Kingdom by: Hay House UK, Ltd.
292B Kensal Rd., London W10 5BE • Phone: 44-20-8962-1230
Fax: 44-20-8962-1239 • www.hayhouse.co.uk

Published and distributed in the Republic of South Africa by: Hay House
SA (Pty), Ltd., P.O. Box 990, Witkoppen 2068 • Phone/Fax: 27-11-467-8904
info@hayhouse.co.za • www.hayhouse.co.za

Published and Distributed in India by: Hay House Publishers India,
Muskaan Complex, Plot No. 3, B-2, Vasant Kunj, New Delhi 110 070
Phone: 91-11-4176-1620 • Fax: 91-11-4176-1630 • www.hayhouse.co.in

Distributed in Canada by: Raincoast • 9050 Shaughnessy St., Vancouver,
B.C. V6P 6E5 • Phone: (604) 323-7100 • Fax: (604) 323-2600

oOo